TEAMERSHIP

BRING YOUR BEST AND BRING OUT THE BEST IN OTHERS ACROSS MULTIPLE TEAMS.

KEEGAN LUITERS

First published in 2022 for Keegan Luiters by

Longueville Media Pty Ltd
PO Box 205
Haberfield NSW 2045 Australia
www.longmedia.com.au
info@longmedia.com.au

Cover and book design by Sh8peshifters
Artwork by Sh8peshifters

Luiters, Keegan
Teamership
ISBN   978-0-6456150-3-6

A catalogue record for this
book is available from the
National Library of Australia

NATIONAL
LIBRARY
OF AUSTRALIA

Disclaimer

TEAMERSHIP

is not followership.
is a form of leadership.
is how an individual contributes
to collective performance.

is the product of two questions.
is a competitive advantage.

supports courageous commitment.

is an adaptive challenge.
is an untapped energy source.

elevates the humanity in our teams.

is a commitment to making together better.
is both challenging and necessary.

makes multiple teams work.
is the most valuable and undervalued
form of leadership in organisations.

is a choice.

This book is designed to support you in making that choice.

For Mum and Dad

For encouraging me to do my best
and bring out the best in others.

CONTENTS

ABOUT THE AUTHOR

Keegan Luiters is an expert in team performance.

He is an author, speaker, coach and facilitator.
Applying evidence-based approaches, Keegan works with individuals, teams and organisations to deliver sustained performance outcomes.

He has spent his life in and around teams, leadership, learning and performance. At various times, Keegan has been a marathon runner, cricket coach and a keen netball supporter – including a sideline dad. His background includes semi-professional cricket with and against some of the best cricketers in Australia and the UK.

These life experiences are complemented by academic and professional experiences. Keegan has a Masters Degree in Business Coaching from Sydney Business School, is currently Program Director for the New Leader Development Program at Melbourne Business School and has written two books: *Team Up* and now, *Teamership*.

Keegan has partnered with a diverse range of organisations to support leadership and team performance including KPMG, Westpac, The ICONIC, Frucor Suntory, Unilever, Toby's Estate, Powershop, Red Energy, Rawson Homes, Nine Entertainment, Sephora, Brighte, Bilue Biogen, Ambu, Agile Australia, Beiersdorf, Delta Group, Verdia and Parramatta Eels among others.

ACKNOWLEDGEMENTS

Writing *Teamership* has been a living lesson in working as a part of multiple teams all committed to the same goal. While it is my name on the cover, there are many people to thank for their support and contribution to this book. Without them, there is no way it would have been in the world in this format and at this time.

I'd like to thank the team that matters most. Thank you to my wife, Rebecca, for all your support – emotional and logistical. Thanks also for your guidance, which has made this book better. Thanks also for putting up with me when I wasn't bringing my best. Thank you to the other member of that team – my daughter, Alia. You bring your best so often and make me want to do the same.

Thank you to David Longfield of Longueville Media who has provided guidance from very early on in the process – every conversation helped the book to become better. Thanks to Alan Chen and Diana Ayoub – also known as Sh8peshifters – for your illustrative genius that is splashed from cover to cover in this book. Love your work. Thank you to Cynthia Colli, the Creative Concierge! Without directly working on the book, you have played a huge part in getting this important message out through your web and graphic design. Thank you to Sireen Assafiri who, as my Practice Manager, has the unenviable task of keeping me on track and on task.

Others have contributed to this book through conversations, suggestions, feedback or testimonials. They include Carolyn Viso, Melitta Hardenberg, Justin Placek, Geoff Martin, Matt Church, Lyndall Bushell, Lisa O'Neill and Tracey Ezard. Thanks to each of you for the time and effort that you have committed to this project.

An important thank you to the leaders, teams and organisations that I work with. It is a privilege to do so. I hope this book helps that work live on further and longer.

A final note of thanks to you, the reader, for reading this book – including the acknowledgements! I appreciate your time and attention and trust that the book will give you clarity on the importance and processes of Teamership.

" Connections are the energy that exists between people when they feel seen, heard, and valued. "

———————————————

Professor Brene Brown

INTRODUCTION

This book exists to start and support important conversations about why and how to be a great team member across multiple teams.

Conversations about being a great team member – particularly in the context of multiple teams – are important because they allow us to identify the assumptions and structures that are holding us back. Despite the fact that 95% of people across industries are on multiple teams, very few approaches exist to support multiple team membership.

There is no doubt that leadership is an important and valuable area for organisations to focus on. In this book, I advocate for leadership as an essential component of supporting the conditions for individuals to make great contributions. Too often, however, there is an overemphasis on the impact of individual leadership that ignores the opportunity of collective leadership. Very few organisations and leaders spend time considering how to help individuals thrive as part of the multiple teams that we all find ourselves working within.

This need to effectively work across multiple teams is emerging more frequently as organisations realise that assumptions born in the Industrial Revolution and baked into their organisational chart are inadequate for the 21st Century. There is a need to shift working towards a more *human, dynamic, networked and systemic* approach.

This book touches on all of these elements. However, at this point, I'd like to focus on the reference to humanity. The need to work across multiple teams feels like a very modern and commercial pursuit. It is my belief, though, that the secret to succeeding across multiple teams is to tap into some of the best and most long established elements of our humanity.

In our lives, from the earliest ages, we have had multiple roles. As child, friend, student, teacher, coach, supporter, sibling, partner and more. As we grow, those roles evolve and so do we. We are built to operate in and across multiple roles. It is the false and imposed constraints of our assumptions in a work setting that have been holding us back.

Throughout our multiple roles and throughout the human experience, there are constants. We achieve remarkable things when we work together in community. Even individual performances rely on direct or indirect collaboration and co-operation from others. At our best, we are lifted up by others and we lift others up.

None of this is to suggest that working in fast paced organisations across multiple roles is easy. It is not. But it is clear that current approaches are insufficient. Working harder and longer will not achieve our objectives. To that point, pushing our people to work harder and longer is a primary driver of the emerging trends of the great resignation and quiet quitting.

If more of the same is not going to keep up with the requirements at individual, team and organisational level, then we need a new way of thinking. It is my sincere hope that you will consider the ideas presented in this book.

They form an approach that I believe acknowledges and celebrates our ability to work collectively and which is designed for sustainable performance.

Teamership is very much a distillation of my experiences, observations, perspectives, and personal research. However, many academic and business research papers also support its contents. I have included a reference list at the back and on its website. If you would like to know more about my experiences or perspectives, please get in touch and we can explore any topic that is covered through the lens of your context.

This is a book designed to start conversations, so at the end of each section you will see a set of reflective questions to help *you bring your best* and a discussion guide to help *you bring out the best in others*. You can use these questions to facilitate discussions with existing teams, leadership groups, and colleagues to explore the concepts of the section.

SECTION 1

WHAT IS
TEAMERSHIP?

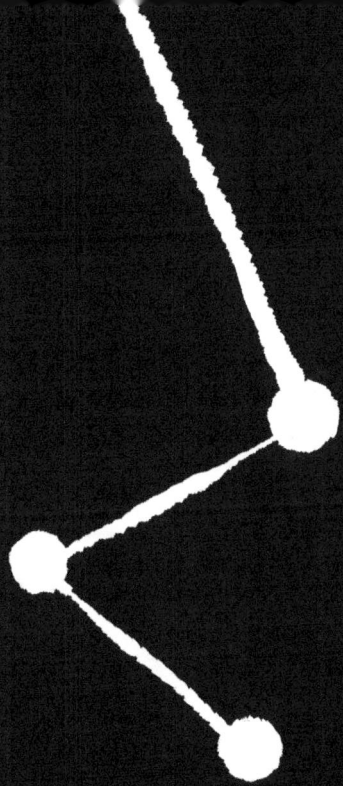

Teamership is not followership.

Teamership is a form of leadership.

Teamership is a competitive advantage.

Teamership is the product
of two questions.

Teamership is a commitment
to making together better.

Teamership is a choice.

I WAS best man at my friend Tim's wedding and vice versa. For our speeches, there were two strict criteria. The first was timing. We were marrying women who could articulate what they wanted succinctly, so we knew we had five minutes! The second was that our speeches needed to include a made-up word.

Tim's word, like his speech, was better than mine – *vaguerise*.

Vaguerise means to "summarise in less detail". It's such a great word and something that needs to happen far more often in many circumstances. How many times have you wished that a presenter had done a better job of vaguerising their slide deck?

My word was happenable.

It was invented by accident. I meant to say feasible or possible and just said *happenable*. It means what it says – something that is able to happen.

There is a reason that I am sharing these stories. This book is centred on another word that I have made up.

Teamership.

Teamership means many things. Distilled, it can be defined as:

The power or ability of an individual to contribute to collective performance.

This first section is dedicated to exploring what Teamership is – and is not. It will help you see that Teamership has been hiding in plain sight and show what a conscious approach to supporting Teamership can offer.

You will read about:

- How Teamership is similar to concepts such as leadership and distinct from other concepts such as followership.
- The two central questions of Teamership
- Considering Teamership as a competitive advantage.

Teamership

/tiːmə.ʃɪp/   noun

The power or ability of an individual to contribute to collective performance.

TEAMERSHIP IS NOT ____
FOLLOWERSHIP

Barbara Kellerman is a Fellow at the Harvard Kennedy School's Centre for Public Leadership and has written extensively about followership. This includes her 2008 book, unsurprisingly titled *Followership*.

Followership is a well considered and researched book that seeks to remove the stigma and shame attached to being a *follower* – a term often used to make others feel small. Many of us remember the shame associated with being labelled a follower at school! Kellerman's book points to the impact that those without official leadership titles are increasingly able to have, citing examples from a range of settings.

Kellerman highlights the limitations and overreach of established approaches to leadership. The book pushes back against the leader-centric views that are often pervasive. I largely agree with both of those points – that the impact of people without a leadership title is undervalued and there is significant risk in overemphasising the leader as a hero.

While there are areas of alignment, there are key differences between Kellerman's and my views on Teamership. This is highlighted by Kellerman's position on followership, which she defines as:

> *"The response of those in subordinate positions (followers) to those in superior ones (leaders). Followership implies a relationship (rank) between subordinates and superiors, and a response (behaviour) of the former to the latter"*

The use of *subordinates* and *superiors* perpetuates a sense of rank and hierarchy that doesn't reflect the complex and dynamic way in which teams operate in modern settings.

In particular, this book challenges the idea of labelling individuals as leaders or followers – which implies that we are either one or the other.

The fact is that at any given time, any of us can take a position of leadership or of followership in service of the team's objectives. One of the most dangerous and limiting approaches that a team can take is to place all of its decision making, accountability and responsibility with one person. It dilutes the impact of the team and reduces the chance that it can perform in a way that is greater than the sum of its parts.

Positioning an individual as a leader or a follower reduces the likelihood that each person brings their best contribution to the team. Teamership is more dynamic than that – sometimes leading, sometimes following. Teamership is always acting in service of the team's purpose.

TEAMERSHIP IS A FORM OF LEADERSHIP

There are many definitions of leadership in both academic and business worlds. Putting "definition, leadership" into Google comes up with almost 1.5 billion hits in 0.52 seconds!

In the context of modern organisations, most of the useful definitions connect leadership with behaviours and actions – and not purely positional authority.

An example from academic literature is from Gary Yukl in 2013, who defines leadership as:

> *"...the process of influencing others to understand and agree about what needs to be done and how to do it, and the process of facilitating individual and collective efforts to accomplish shared objectives.'"*

In the business world, an example comes from Microsoft founder, Bill Gates:

> *"As we look ahead into the next century, leaders will be those who empower others."*

From that, we can imply that Gates' working definition of leadership would be *empowering others.*

Neither Yukl's academic definition nor Gates' commercial definition requires positional authority. This is both an opportunity and a challenge.

In modern organisations, where many teams are absent from the organisational chart, we can't rely on formally appointed leaders and managers to provide all of the necessary leadership. Some teams may have no members with a designated leadership or managerial position. Others, like leadership teams, consist exclusively of 'leaders'. All of these teams benefit from leadership as an act, and a way of behaving that supports collective performance towards meaningful objectives.

Teamership is clearly not about leading with authority or a title. It is about how individuals add value and contribute to the team to serve its purpose. Through this lens, Teamership is more dynamic and responsive than a title or even a set role within a team.

While not the traditional form of leadership that defines strategy, goals, rewards and punishments, Teamership is a form of leadership that drives performance. Teamership is the most valuable – and simultaneously undervalued – form of leadership in organisations.

TEAMERSHIP IS THE PRODUCT OF _____ TWO QUESTIONS

Being a great team member sounds easy. I am willing to bet, however, that it doesn't happen as often as you would like. All of us and those we work with have moments where we are not great team members.

It is a safe assumption that if there was an easy or obvious solution, someone would have figured out how to make it happen. Given that we are dealing with humans, easy and obvious solutions are rare or illusionary.

The fact is that being a great team member is a complex and dynamic task requiring awareness and adaptability. Often, in the midst of complexity, insight can be found through a combination of simple questions and honest answers.

Here are the two questions that I recommend you ask yourself and others.

Am I bringing my best?

Am I bringing out the best in others?

Simple questions. Honest answers to those two questions will give you an insight into your current level of Teamership.

Continuing to put in the effort so that the answer to both of those questions is yes is challenging. It also leads to better outcomes at multiple levels. There is intrinsic reward in being a great team member, which benefits individuals. Better team members contribute positively to team performance. Organisations benefit from teams that are connected and interconnected.

The two questions of Teamership allow us to continually reconnect with the principles of improving collective performance – at individual, team and organisational levels.

AM I BRINGING MY BEST?

AM I BRINGING OUT THE BEST IN OTHERS?

TEAMERSHIP IS A COMPETITIVE ADVANTAGE

According to a resource-based view of strategy, a key part of an organisation's sustained success and competitive advantage is to identify and leverage its capabilities in a way that is difficult for others to imitate or approximate.

I was recently delivering a leadership development program with Melbourne Business School Professor of Strategy, Geoff Martin. He identified several factors that are difficult to imitate. Three were directly connected to Teamership: culture, brand and relationships.

CULTURE

Great culture is not possible without Teamership.

It is possible that groups can achieve incredible *results* without Teamership, but they would not necessarily be positive outcomes for all involved. Our world is littered with examples of human exploitation or control for the benefit of a few.

It is not possible for members of a group to identify their culture as great when the environment does not allow themselves or others to bring their best. A great culture is one where everyone brings their best and allows others to do the same, to achieve a good result for all. Individuals seek to pursue their best possible contribution to collective performance.

BRAND

Brand is typically seen as the external experience of an organisation, whereas culture is the internal experience. There is good reason to link the two. In a 2010 *Harvard Business Review* article, Bill Taylor gives away the punchline in the title: *Brand Is Culture, Culture Is Brand.*

He says "you can't be special, distinctive, and compelling in the marketplace unless you create something special, distinctive, and compelling in the workplace."

And that's where Teamership comes into play. It works on the inside to create the special, distinctive, and compelling workplaces required to deliver you a special, distinctive, and compelling brand.

RELATIONSHIPS

Teamership relies on creating better connections. Establishing, maintaining and strengthening relationships in all areas – with colleagues, with supply chain partners, and with customers – is essential for high levels of Teamership. Without relationships, we are unlikely to bring our best or encourage others to do the same. We need to care about those we work with as humans, not just resources.

Teamership elevates culture, brand and relationships – elements that shape your organisation's competitive advantage.

TEAMERSHIP IS A _____ COMMITMENT TO MAKING TOGETHER BETTER

The phrase *making together better* smacks of a cheesy marketing or political campaign. It can easily sound like fluffy words that are thrown together to sound nice, but don't necessarily mean very much.

For that reason, I'd like to clarify what I mean by *making together better*.

MAKE TOGETHER BETTER THAN SEPARATE

Firstly, making together better is about operating in ways that make working collectively more valuable than working separately. But this is not always the case. Abdullah Almaatouq and his co-authors in a 2021 paper noted that:

"Groups are as fast as the fastest individual and more efficient than the most efficient individual when the task is complex but not when the task is simple".

21

In other words, working together is better when there is complexity involved – which is a lot of the time! The principles of Teamership are critical when we are required to work with others.

MAKING CURRENT WAYS OF WORKING TOGETHER BETTER

Secondly, Teamership is about improving our ways of working together. In spite of the fact that teams are more prevalent in organisations than ever, our experiences in teams and across teams is not always great. In fact, research by Richard Hackman, Ruth Wageman and others has found that only 21% of leadership teams are high performing and 42% perform poorly.

Teamership seeks to improve ways of working – and make working together better in that way.

The final point is that making together better isn't a passive process. It's an ongoing and active process that takes energy, attention and time from all of us.

TEAMERSHIP IS A CHOICE

Organisations that seek great performance rely on individuals consistently making decisions that benefit the organisation's interests – beyond the obligations of their employment contracts. A series of choices contributes to this.

INDIVIDUALS NEED TO CHOOSE TO JOIN, STAY, AND GROW AT YOUR ORGANISATION.

High performing organisations need to attract, retain and develop talented individuals. Organisations are operating in a hyper-competitive employment market with daily articles about the Great Resignation, employee burnout or quiet quitting. This means that there is an advantage in helping individuals to choose to join, stay, and grow at an organisation for reasons beyond their salary.

INDIVIDUALS NEED TO CHOOSE TO BRING THEIR BEST WORK.

High performing organisations can't carry people who are holding back. Talented individuals are a great start, but there are plenty of talented and underperforming individuals in organisations large and small – particularly large ones! An HR director at a large media company told me, "we can't afford people hiding". This means that individuals need to choose to bring their best work.

INDIVIDUALS NEED TO CHOOSE TO BRING THEIR BEST WORK WITHIN A NETWORK OF TEAMS.

High performing individuals are not enough – success is a team sport.

A 2018 issue of the Human Resource Management Review was dedicated to high performance teamwork in organisations. The authors, Thomas O'Neill and Eduardo Salas, cover a range of emerging and evolving challenges around teamwork in organisations. Succinctly and powerfully, they state:

The reality is that teams are needed, they are here to stay.

They highlight the need for addressing large and complex challenges through teamwork – particularly multiple team networks. In that context, they further point out that "interacting with other teams might be just as important as within-team interactions".

While these choices of Teamership are made at an individual level, it is clear that an organisational climate that promotes, supports, and enables Teamership aids these choices.

Will your organisation choose Teamership?

REFLECTIVE QUESTIONS

To help you bring your best

1. How do *you* define Teamership?

2. In what ways do you think that Teamership is different, or similar, to followership?

3. In what ways do you think that Teamership is different, or similar, to leadership?

4. How do you bring your best to your roles in teams?

5. What do you do to bring out the best in others?

6. How do others bring out the best in you?

7. Have you noticed anything that makes it hard for you to bring your best?

8. When do your teams need you to lead – even without a leadership title?

9. How are you recharging yourself so that you can turn up as a good version of you?

10. Teamership is ...

The power or ability of an individual to contribute to collective performance.

On a scale of 1 (exceptionally low) to 10 (exceptionally high), what is your current level of Teamership?

DISCUSSION GUIDE

To help bring out the best in others

1. What is each member's current experience of being a part of this team?

2. Are we supporting the best performance of each member?

3. Are we supporting the best interactions between members?

4. Can we build the agility that allows both team and individual work?

5. Do we collectively support each individual to perform at their best?

6. When do we find ourselves being less productive despite working together?

7. When are we more productive because of working together?

8. How often are we at our best?

9. How can we better support each other?

10. Teamership is...

The power or ability of an individual to contribute to collective performance.

On a scale of 1 (exceptionally low) to 10 (exceptionally high), what is our current level of Teamership?

SECTION II

WHY TEAMERSHIP? WHY NOW?

Your org chart is lying to you.

Product v. Packshot

Shifting to a team-based network model improves performance.

93% of organisations aren't ready to operate as networks.

The rise of multiple team members.

Individuals on multiple teams are overcommitted.

THE WORLD that our organisations operate in is hyper-connected. Sharing information, ideas and culture is occurring at rates that dwarf previous levels of interaction – and this trend is set to continue. Unless our organisations operate in a way that matches this level of interconnectivity, they won't keep pace with the environment in which they exist. Many organisations are aware of this and are seeking to make structural changes to their ways of working.

A 2019 report by global consultancy, Deloitte, calls organisational performance a 'team sport'. In other words, the competitiveness of organisations in the current and emerging climate relies on the ability to operate in a network of teams. The Deloitte research picked up some interesting trends – in particular, the huge gap between the opportunity presented by working through teams and the current reality.

The shift from 'functional hierarchy to team-centric and network-based organisational models' was viewed as important or very important by 65% of the survey respondents — but only 7% felt very ready to execute this shift.

That is fascinating to consider.

A total of 93% of organisations were not fully ready to operate in a network-based model

It is clear that organisations have changed the way that they would like to work. Many have made structural changes within their organisations. As a result, the vast majority of people in knowledge working roles are on multiple teams. That is an indication that organisations are shifting from pure hierarchies.

These structural changes are helpful, yet insufficient.

The missing piece is that a network based model requires something different from each of those within the organisation. Making multiple teams work requires a shift in skillsets and mindsets so that everyone makes a positive contribution to the collective performance across their multiple teams.

The power or ability of individuals to contribute to collective performance – which is literally the definition of Teamership – is the missing piece.

Teamership matters. Now more than ever.

In this section, you will read about:

- The gap between your org chart and what is required in modern organisations
- The value of a dynamic network of human systems
- The rise of multiple team membership – and the need to avoid overcommitment across teams.

YOUR ORG CHART IS LYING TO YOU

Organisational charts don't reflect the way that teams operate within organisations. A global study by ADP Research Institute in 2018 backs this up. Its report stated that of the 19 346 respondents ...

75 percent report that the teams they are on are not represented in the organisational chart.

In a 2019 Harvard Business Review article titled "The Power of Hidden Teams", the authors of this research, Marcus Buckingham and Ashley Goodall, say that teams are not defined by an org chart showing who reports to whom in which department. They note that:

> *"[Teams] emerge from a multitude of requests and acceptances, none of which HR sees, some of which are overlapping, many of which are ephemeral, and all of which are where people's actual experience of work truly resides."*

Individually, this means that our position title / job description / email signature / LinkedIn profile doesn't match our actual roles at work. Collectively, this means that the expectations of individuals' ability to operate across multiple teams is a long way ahead of how our organisations are formally structured or our systems are designed to support.

This presents a challenge.

If we individually and collectively are unable to identify and acknowledge these phantom teams, we are fighting an uphill battle. We will use tools, approaches and beliefs that are contrary to the current reality. That will mean that we miss huge opportunities for improving the experience of working together and fail to leverage the best talent available.

In contrast, by acknowledging and labelling all the work we do and the teams we are in, we create a realistic picture of who we are and what work we do. To acknowledge that we all work in a multiple team environment means we will be better able to attract, retain, develop and leverage the best talent – a huge competitive advantage for our organisation.

How your org chart tells you that work gets done.

How work really gets done.

PRODUCT VS. _____
PACKSHOT

In Australia, our national broadcaster, the ABC, used to run a consumer affairs show called 'The Checkout'. It was intended to help us be better consumers – and keep companies on their toes! One segment that I always enjoyed was *Product vs. Packshot*.

It was a segment that, ironically enough, did what it said. It compared a real life image of a product – often sent in by a viewer – with the image presented in the product's marketing material. These were often frozen meals or kids' toys and the product bore little to no resemblance to the image presented.

If we look at how work (the 'product') gets done in organisations – compared to the assumptions implied through the organisational chart (the 'packshot'), we also see that the reality does not align with the image.

STATIC VS. DYNAMIC

The organisational chart assumes that the operating environment is static. Organisations are, in fact, dynamic – always changing. Organisations are both influenced by and have an influence on the context in which they are operating.

HIERARCHY VS. NETWORK

The organisational chart assumes that the best structure is a hierarchy because it has centralised command and control where leaders decide and others execute orders. Reality requires a decentralised network that allows for empowered execution throughout the organisation.

This reality is not to be confused with a lack of structure – networks still have structure, but don't possess the bottlenecks of hierarchical structures.

HUMANS VS. RESOURCES

An organisational chart implies that people are resources.

Resources are consistent, mechanical and excellent at repeating prescribed tasks. Humans are irrational and idiosyncratic. The inconsistency of humans makes us mediocre as resources. Repetitive tasks requiring little thought are best for resources. Humans are better suited to tasks where there is the need to coordinate, collaborate and overcome challenges that are not able to be solved by following a set of instructions. This is the beauty of harnessing human capabilities and it is what organisations need more of. Why waste humans on menial repetitive tasks when our capabilities are so unique and irreplaceable by a machine?

MECHANICAL VS. SYSTEMIC SOLUTIONS

An organisational chart's separate components and streams imply that solutions are technical in nature.

Technical challenges can be solved by existing knowledge and capabilities in a logical progression. An airline with a malfunctioning engine is faced with a technical challenge that someone with sufficient mechanical knowledge and expertise can repair. Technical challenges require mechanical solutions.

If the same airline was trying to figure out why customer satisfaction is declining, they face a more complex challenge possibly without a clear answer. Customer satisfaction for an airline is the product of a number of variables – such as passenger comfort, pricing, customer service, on time departures, safety and many more – interacting with one another. Looking at a component of customer satisfaction in isolation could easily make things worse. A focus on cutting prices could reduce staff numbers, which could lead to lower service levels. Improving on time departures could mean a reduced emphasis on safety. Customer satisfaction needs to be considered collectively.

Systemic challenges need to be considered as a whole – considering the components of the system, as well as the interactions of those components. Organisations need ways of working that allow them to respond to systemic challenges holistically. To do this, better connections within the organisation are needed. Traditional organisational charts seek to remove those connections, preferring an assumption that all challenges can be resolved through the components of the system, rather than the connections.

YOUR ORG CHART

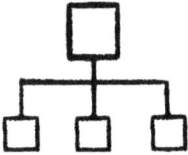

YOUR ORG NEEDS

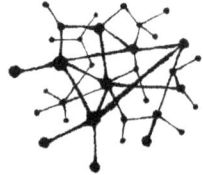

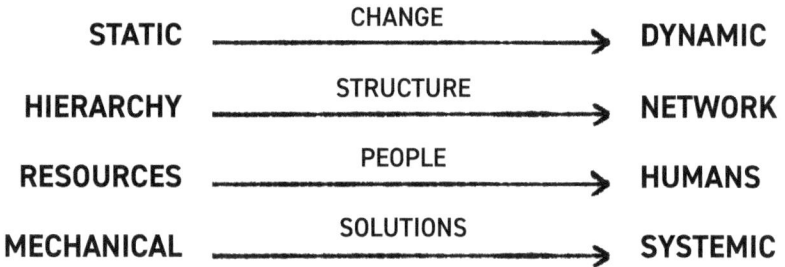

STATIC	CHANGE →	**DYNAMIC**
HIERARCHY	STRUCTURE →	**NETWORK**
RESOURCES	PEOPLE →	**HUMANS**
MECHANICAL	SOLUTIONS →	**SYSTEMIC**

SHIFTING TO A TEAM-BASED NETWORK MODEL IMPROVES PERFORMANCE

Research data in a 2019 report by global consultancy Deloitte highlights some interesting opportunities and gaps. Aligned to the preceding points made in this book, the data suggests that current rates of change mean that the effectiveness of hierarchies is limited.

The report states that *shifting toward a team-based organizational model improves performance, often significantly.* The overwhelming majority (74%) of organisations that are at least partially operating as a team-based network are seeing improvements in performance. A total of 53% of respondents reported that operating as a team-based network had led to a *significant improvement in performance.*

This is supported in other areas of both academic and business literature. Another global consultancy, McKinsey, during the early months of the COVID-19 pandemic echoed Deloitte's research. McKinsey stated that the way to operate in the face of a rapidly changing situation was *a robust network of teams that is empowered to operate outside of the current hierarchy and bureaucratic structures of the organisation.*

In academic literature, there is increased attention on multiple team systems. In 2015, Marissa Shuffler and William Kramer found that *multiple team systems are critical to current and future organizational success*. A 2019 review of the previous decade's research into team effectiveness by John Mathieu and others found organisations *have adopted team-based designs to maximize the value of their human capital*. A 2020 review by Jaclyn Margolis similarly found that multiple team networks improved effectiveness when the conditions were correct.

These academic findings reinforce the trend towards multiple team networks that has been increasing over the past decade or two. The caveat is that success in a multiple team environment requires a shift in ways of working. How to implement this shift in a way that supports success in a multiple team environment is described throughout this book – in most detail in the sections titled *Designing Teamership* and *Integrating Teamership*.

93% OF ORGANISATIONS AREN'T READY TO OPERATE AS NETWORKS

While there is a desire and awareness of the benefits of a team-based network, Deloitte's research picked up some interesting trends – in particular, the gap between the opportunity presented by working through teams and the current reality.

There is a huge gap between these aspirations and reality. The report states that:

> *"Sixty-five percent of this year's survey respondents viewed the shift from 'functional hierarchy to team-centric and network-based organizational models' as important or very important – but only 7 percent of respondents felt very ready to execute this shift, and only 6 percent rated themselves very effective at managing cross-functional teams."*

This emphasises two things. Firstly, that a desire to be able to operate in a more team based network does not, in itself, provide the competitive advantage that many organisations seek. This leads to the second point: that finding a way to improve your capability to operate in a network can and will set you ahead of the curve.

THE RISE OF MULTIPLE TEAM MEMBERSHIP

In spite of what our organisational charts say, the reality for most people in knowledge working roles – what we might have called *office jobs* in those pre-COVID days – is that they are on more than one team. Research from the Centre for Creative Leadership found that 95% of people across a range of industries are on more than one team at a time. Anecdotally, it is very rare to meet someone who is on only one team.

A senior learning professional at SEEK, a market leader in online employment marketplaces operating in the Asia Pacific and Latin America, estimates that across their business, every individual is on an average of 3.2 teams. I suspect that this is under-reported. My experience in speaking to people in a range of industries and organisations is that most people cannot readily identify all of the teams that they are a part of.

As organisations shift to operate as a dynamic network of teams, individuals will continue to find themselves on more and more teams. To estimate the number of teams in which they operate, we need to look at the following:

HIERARCHY

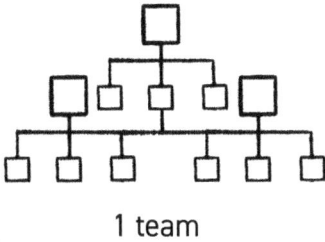

1 team

In a *pure* hierarchy where there are clear lines of responsibility and no cross-functional connections, most individuals are on *one team*.

MATRIX

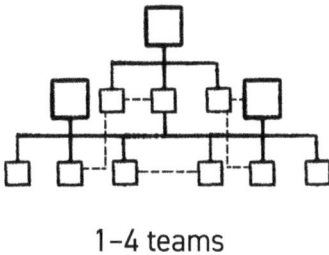

1–4 teams

In a matrix organisational structure, the inclusion of "dotted line" or latticed reporting lines means that individuals are on somewhere *between one and four teams*.

NETWORK

5–12+ teams

In a team-based network, it is common for an individual to be a member of *five, ten, or twelve or more teams at a time*.

The rise of multiple team membership amplifies the need and value of great team members. They're required to have a more responsive and flexible way of working than has been demanded previously.

INDIVIDUALS ON MULTIPLE TEAMS ARE OVERCOMMITTED

In "The Overcommitted Organisation", a 2017 *Harvard Business Review* article by Mark Mortensen and Heidi Gardner, the central premise was that individuals in are increasingly on multiple teams and are stretched too thin to do their work well. This leads organisations to operate at an unsustainable pace and with too few employees to deliver their best work.

Overcommitted employees means a high risk of negative outcomes:

- Organisations will not be able to deliver on promises to themselves, their customers, and their stakeholders.

- Teams will increasingly need to achieve more with less formal or informal support and fewer resources.

- Individuals risk burning out or languishing as they simply can't keep pace.

The potential benefits of multiple team membership are significant. It leads to a more responsive organisation, better utilisation of people's capabilities, higher levels of engagement and knowledge transfer, and a greater ability to adapt to complex challenges. There is a risk that without proper support and design, this multiple team membership model can lead to worse outcomes, but the solution is not a return to more hierarchy and structure.

Investment is needed for organisations to experience the benefits of multiple team membership. Beyond words or slogans, organisations need to be committed to making a network a sustainable way of working. The benefits to the organisation need to be carefully weighed against the implications for individuals to avoid employees becoming overcommitted and less productive.

REFLECTIVE QUESTIONS

To help you bring your best

These questions are designed to help you consider how you can bring your best to the teams that you are part of, and particularly why Teamership matters in your role.

1. How many teams are you part of?

2. Can you articulate the purpose of each team that you are part of?

3. How many of your current teams are visible on the organisational chart?

4. What are your roles across your multiple teams?

5. How often do you feel overcommitted across multiple teams?

6. In what ways have your teams changed in the past 1, 5, 10, or 20 years?

7. How do you add strength to your teams?

8. How do your teams add strength to you?

9. What would happen if you and everyone you worked with were just 1% better at being a team member?

10. What is one way that you can help others that you work with at the moment?

DISCUSSION GUIDE

To help bring out the best in others

1. How prepared are we to operate as a part of a team based network?

2. What current practices support a team based network?

3. Are any assumptions holding us back from working together better?

4. How often are we at our best collectively?

5. In what ways has our operating environment changed in the past 1, 5, 10 or 20 years?

6. Are our ways of working more accurately described as static or dynamic?

7. Are we functioning as a hierarchy, matrix or network?

8. Do we need to operate as a hierarchy, matrix or network?

9. Are people in our teams treated as resources or humans?

10. Is our approach best suited for mechanical or systemic solutions?

SECTION III

THE IMPACT OF TEAMERSHIP

Teamership impacts culture and vice versa.

Teamership supports collaboration.

Teamership supports resilience.

Teamership promotes shared leadership.

Teamership prioritises learning.

Teamership is an untapped energy source.

AS WE have seen in previous sections, high levels of Teamership are important for organisational success. The rapid rates of change experienced by organisations need more than structural changes. To make the most of the benefits of operating as a team based network requires behavioural changes at individual, leader, team and organisational levels.

A team based network is desirable for many reasons but it can challenge long held assumptions and structures within organisations. Operating as a network requires an ability to shift from the mindsets that underpin and promote hierarchy.

Hierarchy gives us a sense of order and control. It gives us a sense of security and confidence. That sense is also an illusion. In complex environments there are indirect links between cause and effect, which means that we can only ever have indirect influence, not direct control. Leading through control creates a bottleneck for modern organisations that need to be led through context – where purpose and performance are prioritised over power and policies.

In a hierarchy, where people are on one team, the level of Teamership required is low. Individuals need only to follow the instructions or rules they are given. More dynamic environments benefit from shared leadership, where leadership responsibilities are distributed within a group and not centralised to the hierarchical leader.

A team-based network, where individuals are on many teams simultaneously needs a high level of Teamership. The more people are able to be their best and bring out the best in others, adapting their approach across the changing contexts of their multiple teams, the better.

The ability of an individual to contribute to collective performance is what allows the benefits of the network to be realised. Quite literally ...

Teamership makes multiple teams work.

Teamership is the way of working that supports a more agile, connected and dynamic organisation. High levels of Teamership can be connected to improvements in organisational performance, culture, levels of collaboration, response to change, and learning orientation.

This section explores:

- The relationship between Teamership and organisational culture

- How Teamership is connected to improved ways of working required in a team based network

- Teamership as a source of energy.

TEAMERSHIP IMPACTS CULTURE
AND VICE VERSA

In the first section of this book, I asserted that a great culture is not possible without Teamership. This seems like an audacious claim. However, it is one that I am confident of within certain bounds.

In academic and business writing, there is no single agreed definition of *culture*. Many have similar traits – some are complex and some are simpler. For our purposes, I have chosen the definition presented in 2016, by Christian van Nieuwerbergh, who said culture was *the generally accepted beliefs, conventions, customs, social norms and behaviours of people who self-identify as members of a particular group.*

With that definition in mind, I have applied Dr Ron Westrum's classification of cultures into three types: pathological, bureaucratic, and generative. His classifications use the way that information flows as a key indicator of a culture.

PATHOLOGICAL

In a pathological culture, information is used to control others. Information is shared only when it serves the interests of the person with the information. Extrapolating this beyond information, there is an orientation towards power – individuals seek to gain, retain and exploit power.

BUREAUCRATIC

Bureaucratic organisations share information through established channels and lines of reporting. In such cultures, there are clear methods of communication and protocols about who is given what type of information. This typically leads to a focus on departmental turf and lines of reporting. Bureaucratic organisations rely heavily on rules and policies.

GENERATIVE

In generative organisations, information flows freely. The people who need information to act in the interest of the organisation can obtain that information. While there are policies and formal lines of communication, communication regularly crosses departmental or organisational lines as required. Generative organisations focus on the organisation's purpose and context. In these cultures, there is an orientation towards performance.

High levels of Teamership support a culture that is focused on performance. Likewise, a generative culture supports, promotes and values high levels of Teamership.

TEAMERSHIP SUPPORTS COLLABORATION

A paradox of Teamership is that it requires us to focus on our own performance as well as that of others. We need to focus on our own performance to do our best, and pay attention to others' to support their best. Getting this balance wrong can have negative impacts for individuals, teams and organisations.

High levels of Teamership require individuals to be able to align and merge our interests with those of others. Applying a simplified approach to a concept presented by Randall Peterson and Kristin Behfar in a 2022 *Harvard Business Review* article, we can see that Teamership supports interactions that shift away from competition, move beyond co-operation and become collaborative. This transition from self to team can be seen in the following:

COMPETITIVE

In competitive relationships, we assume our interactions are a zero-sum game. For one person to win, the other must lose. It stands to reason then, that in these relationships, we will focus on protecting or advancing self-interest.

CO-OPERATIVE

In co-operative relationships, an underlying assumption is that there is some benefit in individuals working together. That benefit lies in situations of mutual self-interest. Beyond that, individuals will also avoid acting against the interests of others. It is a functional and transactional relationship where we complete tasks as requested and required but maintain self-interest.

COLLABORATIVE

Collaborative relationships extend cooperative work and there is an investment in the value of the relationship. In a collaborative relationship, intrinsic value is placed upon the relationship – beyond transactional value – which allows for the discovery and emergence of mutual interests.

High levels of Teamership require us to be collaborative. When we are able to genuinely merge our interests with the interests of others, it delivers mutual benefit and becomes a more sustainable way to operate.

TEAMERSHIP SUPPORTS RESILIENCE

The magnitude, scale and speed of change that organisations are facing is a driving force to shift away from hierarchies towards team-based networks. While there are many definitions of resilience, it is generally seen as allowing someone (or something) to return to its intended purpose, structure and operation after experiencing change or disruption.

Unfortunately, resilience has become a buzzword, on occasion used to imply that an individual is somehow internally deficient if they can't handle what is expected of them. Resilience also feels like something that has become an individual, rather than a collective concern.

Viewing resilience as a collective concern allows more opportunities for people to seek and provide assistance in the face of constant change. As Adam Grant says in his book, *Give and Take*, 'three decades of research show that receiving support from colleagues is a robust antidote to burnout.' Below are three approaches to change within organisations.

RESISTANT

A common approach is to seek to minimise change and its impact. With such an approach, change is viewed as a threat to our way of working. Resulting actions range from denying its presence, which can quickly lead to obsolescence, through to downplaying the magnitude, rate or impact of change – which can lead to late and insufficient responses to the change.

ROBUST

A robust approach acknowledges that change is a constant presence in our world. Such an approach is designed to accommodate change within current ways of working. A defining feature of a robust approach is that the scope of change in which performance can be maintained is bound by specific parameters. Beyond those limits, there is a significant impact on performance.

RESILIENT

A resilient approach not only acknowledges that change is constant but that accurately predicting what changes will emerge is unlikely. The resilient organisation develops the capacity to respond and adapt to changes to the point where it is a strength of their operations.

A central component of Teamership is the need to support the performance of others. This directly impacts on their ability to absorb change without burning out. This mutual support makes individuals, teams and organisations less resistant to change and more resilient.

TEAMERSHIP PROMOTES SHARED LEADERSHIP

Research shows that shared leadership is a benefit for high performing teams. A 2014 meta-analysis by Lauren D'Innocenzo and others supports the positive relationship between shared leadership and team performance. For that to take place, it requires individuals to be able to identify and respond to opportunities for both leadership and followership – often in the space of a short time.

Using the same principles, it is possible to extrapolate this concept to an organisational level to see what this could look like in a multiple team environment. Listed below are ways to consider different approaches to leadership – moving from centralised to shared.

CENTRALISED

When leadership is centralised, leadership responsibilities are concentrated at the top of the organisation. There is an implied belief that the most senior leaders are best placed to make the most important decisions. This approach is driven by power and compliance, where senior leaders control and others comply.

ALLOCATED

When leadership responsibilities are allocated, leadership exists through positional authority with responsibilities given to appointed managers with clear areas of accountability. This approach is driven by permission and control. Those who are allocated leadership responsibilities are granted permission to lead within specified bounds. This control extends to the way in which they lead others.

SHARED

With shared leadership, responsibilities can be assumed by anyone within the organisation based on their ability to contribute to the organisation's purpose. There is a tacit acknowledgement that there may be many people within an organisation who, given their experience, connection with customers, established relationships or unique perspective can contribute to the organisation's mission. This approach is driven by purpose and context. Shared leadership does not rely on an organisational chart, but empowers individuals to empower others in serving the organisation's goals.

Teamership is a form of leadership that relies on the capacity of individuals to respond to situational requirements. Individuals' willingness to both lead and follow is increasingly important as teams and organisations respond to an increasingly complex and changing operating environment.

TEAMERSHIP PRIORITISES LEARNING

In a rapidly changing environment where complete information to make decisions and take actions is a luxury, it is highly likely that errors will occur. Applying a distinction from Westrum's study of cultures [See page 57: Teamership impacts culture and vice versa], I have correlated Teamership with how cultures respond to the failure that is an inherent and unavoidable part of operating in complexity.

BLAME

With low Teamership we cannot bring our best or bring out the best in others. One of the impacts of this is that when things go wrong individuals will tend to avoid accountability. In that type of environment, there is a preference for others to be held accountable. Individuals' primary concern is for their own performance and reputation, not that of others.

JUSTICE

With moderate levels of Teamership there is an inconsistent level of engagement with the collective performance. Typically, there is a desire to do a good job as long as it doesn't disrupt the status quo too much. As such, when things go wrong, individuals seek to ensure that those responsible are managed appropriately. There is a desire for the rules and policies that have been established to be applied.

LEARNING

With high levels of Teamership, individuals are constantly focused on the two questions of Teamership – whether they are bringing their best and bringing out the best in others. With high collective performance as the priority, when things go wrong, individual blame is low. Individuals acknowledge the errors, share them, learn from them and adapt to improve their performance.

Teamership relies on learning and promotes learning. **Great team members are always learning and developing their capabilities as a part of their role at the same time as sharing what they are learning across their multiple teams.**

THE IMPACT OF TEAMERSHIP

TYPE OF ORGANISATIONAL STRUCTURE	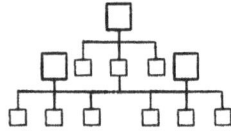 **HIERARCHY**
TEAMERSHIP LEVEL NUMBER OF TEAMS	 LOW 1
CULTURE	 POWER
INTERACTIONS	 COMPETETIVE
RESPONSE TO CHANGE	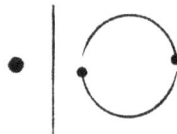 RESISTANT

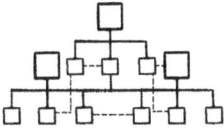 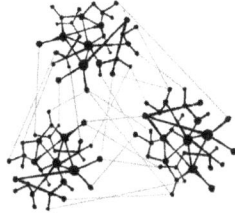

MATRIX **NETWORK**

MODERATE HIGH
1–4 5–12+

POLICIES PERFORMANCE

COOPERATIVE COLLABORATIVE

 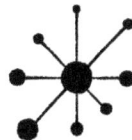

ROBUST RESILIENT

TEAMERSHIP IS AN UNTAPPED
ENERGY SOURCE

In their book, *Time, Talent and Energy*, Michael Mankins and Eric Garton suggest "the more energy people bring to the workplace, the higher the quality of output they produce". It is difficult to argue with that, so let's assume it is true – and connect energy with the role of Teamership. [See also page 99: *Energised Individuals*]

As a concept, energy at work it is unsurprisingly complex. Energy at work is influenced by factors that range from physical (such as working conditions), physiological (including sleep and diet), psychological (motivation among others) and interpersonal factors. For the purposes of considering energy and Teamership, it is important to note the role of interpersonal factors.

I am sure we have all had the experience of being energised by those around us in some way, so let's harness that in the context of how Teamership gives more energy – to individuals, teams and organisations.

TEAMERSHIP GENERATES ENERGY FOR INDIVIDUALS

Consistently, being a part of a team that is performing well – beyond achieving outcomes – is an engaging experience. For over two decades, research has found statistically significant positive correlations between team-based work and a sense of belonging, job satisfaction, empowerment, commitment, and citizenship behaviour. All of these benefits are amplified and made more likely when individuals are actively bringing their best to teams and bringing out the best in their colleagues.

TEAMERSHIP CREATES MAGNETIC ENERGY FOR TEAMS

Beyond the inherent benefits of great team members on team performance, supporting them serves teams in other ways. Most notably, when great team membership behaviours thrive, other great team members are attracted. It also makes the team more likely to be engaged by other teams or clients because the practices of being a great team member mirror those of being a great supplier, partner or client.

TEAMERSHIP RADIATES ENERGY ACROSS THE ORGANISATION

One of the risks of closely knit teams is that they inadvertently become exclusive enclaves that guard their people, expertise, and way of working. When Teamership is at its best, a mindset of abundance is pervasive. Individuals not only bring their best, but focus on helping others to do the same. Given that multiple team membership is the norm, that means that Teamership practices can and do create positive ripples and connections across organisations.

REFLECTIVE QUESTIONS

To help you bring your best

These questions are designed to help you to consider how you can better bring your best to the teams that you are part of, particularly considering the question of why Teamership matters now in your role.

1. Is being a member of multiple teams most often energising or draining for you?

2. What are the things that make being a member of multiple teams energising?

3. Are there times that you notice being a member of multiple teams being draining?

4. Which signals do you send in your teams to show others that they belong?

5. What stops you from being courageous more often?

6. How well do you serve your teams by following the lead of others?

7. Can you imagine a great culture in which members do not demonstrate the values of bringing their best and bringing out the best in others?

8. What can you do to support learning in your teams?

9. Could paying more attention to great team members be valuable for you and your teams?

10. When was the last time you spread joy in your teams?

DISCUSSION GUIDE

To help bring out the best in others

Along each of the following continuums, please mark your current and desired ways of working.

- Mark where you are currently performing with X
- Mark where you would like to be performing with O

OUR NEED FOR TEAMERSHIP IS...

LOW	MEDIUM	HIGH
Most people are on one team	Most people are on 4 or fewer teams	Most people are on 5 or more teams

WE HAVE A CULTURAL FOCUS ON...

POWER	POLICIES	PERFORMANCE
Individuals seek to gain, retain and exploit power.	We rely heavily on rules and policies.	We focus on the organisation's purpose and context.

OUR INTERACTIONS WITH COLLEAGUES ARE TYPICALLY...

COMPETITIVE	CO-OPERATIVE	COLLABORATIVE
We focus on protecting or advancing self-interest.	We complete tasks as requested and required but maintain self-interest.	We enable the discovery and emergence of mutual interests.

LEADERSHIP RESPONSIBILITIES ARE...

CENTRALISED	ALLOCATED	SHARED
Leadership responsibilities are concentrated with the most senior leaders.	Leadership exists through positional authority with responsibilities given to appointed managers.	Leadership responsibilities can be assumed by anyone based on their ability to contribute to the organisation's purpose.

MOST OFTEN, WHEN ERRORS OCCUR, WE SEEK...

BLAME	JUSTICE	LEARNING
Individuals' primary concern is for their own performance and reputation, not that of others.	Individuals seek to ensure that those responsible are managed appropriately through established rules and policies.	Individuals acknowledge the errors, share them, learn from them, and adapt to improve their performance.

WHEN CHANGE IMPACTS US, WE ARE...

RESISTANT	ROBUST	RESILIENT
Our response to change is typically late and insufficient.	We deal well with expected changes and poorly with unexpected changes.	Our strength is that we respond and adapt to changes.

SECTION IV

DESIGNING
TEAMERSHIP

Behaviour is a function of the person and their environment.

Teamership is an adaptive challenge.

An organisational network needs a Teamership network.

Connected Leadership Teams.

Dynamic Leadership capability.

Energised Individuals.

Energised Individuals bring their best and bring out the best in others.

IN 2015, I heard Dan Gregory of The Behaviour Report present at an event. Among the pearls of wisdom were three words that took me about a year and a half to fully appreciate. They were:

Design beats discipline.

I suspect that part of my delay in grasping the concept was driven by a resistance to the message. I wanted to believe that everything I had achieved was because I worked hard. I wanted to believe that I could pursue goals and make changes in my life purely through the force of my willpower. I wanted to believe that for others as well.

With Gregory's words floating somewhere in the back of my mind, I came to see their value. I started to make sense of the message. To make sustainable changes in our ways of living and working, willpower works – to a point. It is, however, an energy intensive and volatile strategy.

Teamership requires a behavioural shift at individual, team, and organisational levels. As with any behaviour change, it is a complex process that requires not only a desire to shift, but also an environment that assists.

While it still takes effort, design is a more sustainable and reliable method of making change. For instance, a client of mine, Sarah, told me that if she wants to go for a run in the morning, she goes to bed in her running outfit! That piece of design significantly increases the chances of her desired behaviour of a run in the morning. Sarah had learnt that relying on her willpower or discipline alone was less effective than designing a solution that made her desired behaviour more likely.

This principle applies in our personal lives often. If you want to stop eating chocolate, it is easier not to have chocolate in the house, which is a design decision, than it is to rely on not eating chocolate that is readily available, which relies on discipline. Making a design choice is not only easier, it is also more likely to succeed.

In the context of Teamership, design involves appreciating the influence of the physical and social environment on behaviour. It means thinking through what elements that environment needs to contain and how to move beyond mandating behaviours, which relies on discipline, and moving towards *nudging* the desired behaviours through design.

According to Nobel Prize Winner Richard Thaler and co-author Cass Sunstein, a nudge is a process of encouraging a desired behaviour without removing free choice. They go on to say:

> *"Nudges are not mandates. Putting the fruit at eye level counts as a nudge. Banning junk food does not."*

It might be tempting to mandate Teamership through rules and policies, however this leads to the kind of top-down management that Teamership is aiming to overcome. We want to encourage, support, and promote the behaviours that support Teamership.

This section examines:

- How to apply the second law of human behaviour

- The ecosystem that fosters Teamership

- What Teamership requires from leadership teams, leaders and individuals.

BEHAVIOUR_____

IS A FUNCTION OF THE PERSON AND THEIR ENVIRONMENT

Aline Holzwarth, Principal of the wonderfully named Centre for Advanced Hindsight at Duke University, published an article on behavioraleconomics.com that presented three laws of human behaviour.

You may want to think of them as principles rather than laws, but either way, they are very helpful to keep in mind when working with humans. They are based on Newton's laws of motion that you might remember from high school physics:

1. A body remains at rest, or in motion at a constant speed in a straight line, unless acted upon by a force.

2. When a body is acted upon by a force, the time rate of change of its momentum equals the force.

3. If two bodies exert forces on each other, these forces have the same magnitude but opposite directions.

We don't need to examine each of Holzwarth's laws here, because I want to focus on the second:

Behaviour is a function of the person and their environment

While behavioural economics feels like a very 21st century endeavour, my friend, Juan shared research that shows this 'Law' can be traced back at least as far as the work of the psychologist Kurt Lewin in the early 20th century. My observation is that we typically overemphasise the person and underemphasise the environment.

When people are not performing in the way that we would like them to, we often assume it is because of something that they are responsible for, such as their lack of skill, motivation, discipline, or organisation. The second law of human behaviour doesn't exclude personal influences as a factor but does ask us to consider what influence their environment has on their performance.

The same occurs on the inverse scenario. When we are seeing a performance that is above our expectations, we can often overemphasise the role of the individual in the performance. We often assume that it is due to their intelligence, efforts and resilience, which can lead us to underestimate the role of the environment – their resources, organisational support or other team members.

The second law helps remind us that Teamership is more likely to occur in an environment that supports, promotes, rewards and encourages those behaviours that allow us to bring our best and bring out the best in others.

TEAMERSHIP IS AN _____
ADAPTIVE CHALLENGE

Ronald Heifetz of Harvard Business School differentiates challenges into categories of technical and adaptive.

Technical challenges can be solved with existing knowledge and capabilities, such as our faulty jet engine from page 37 [Product v Packshot]. There is a "right" answer to the challenge. It has been replicated or approximated previously and can be resolved through applying the right skillsets.

In contrast, adaptive challenges are systemic. Adaptive challenges do not have one clear and correct answer. In fact, adaptive challenges often take a long time to properly define in the first place and the question can be as hard to articulate as the solution. Adaptive challenges are more complex challenges that require a response that shifts the status quo. Responding to adaptive challenges requires improvements in both skillsets and mindsets.

Teamership is an adaptive challenge. Bringing our best and bringing out the best in others across multiple teams requires us to change behaviours. As tempting as it may be to believe, simply supporting those behaviours by developing skills or providing knowledge will be a short term fix at best. Truly shifting towards Teamership behaviour in the long run requires understanding the dynamics, assumptions and mindsets that lead to those behaviours. Behaviour change is more likely when our beliefs and the environment are conducive to the new behaviours.

When we look at supporting Teamership, it is worth keeping more of Heifetz's words in mind ...

" *The most common mistake in leadership is trying to solve an adaptive problem with a technical solution.* "

Ronald Heifetz

AN ORGANISATIONAL NETWORK NEEDS A TEAMERSHIP NETWORK

Given that behaviour is a function of the person and their environment, it makes sense to pay attention to the environment. A useful way to consider this is that operating as an organisational network requires a network of Teamership.

In a network, there is value not only in the components but also the connections between those components. Improving one component of a network will lead to limited benefits. To generate changes that are longer lasting and more widespread, it's important to consider all of the components of a network *and* their integration. How well the components share information, resources, energy and so on is a measure of how far a network under- or outperforms the capacity of independent operation of its components.

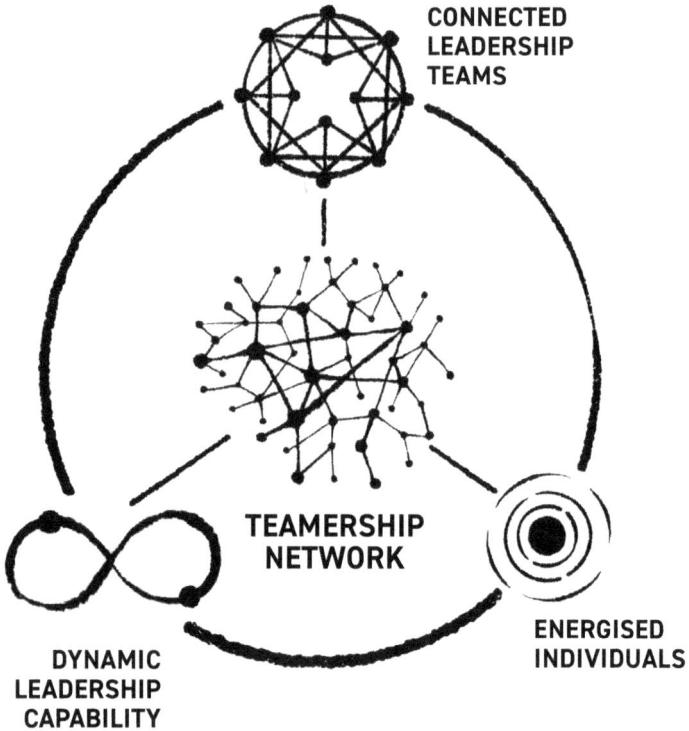

CONNECTED
LEADERSHIP
TEAMS

TEAMERSHIP
NETWORK

ENERGISED
INDIVIDUALS

DYNAMIC
LEADERSHIP
CAPABILITY

The internet operates like this in many ways. A computer by itself without an internet connection can perform some useful tasks, but it suffers severe limitations. When it is connected to the internet, it can do a lot more with greater access to information, resources and updated software. When the computer is connected to the network, we can also add value to the network with information, interactions and so on.

My point is that while I have separated the components of the Teamership network for clarification, organisations see the greatest benefits when they are integrated. An organisational environment that supports, promotes, rewards and encourages Teamership contains three key components:

1. Connected Leadership Teams

2. Dynamic Leadership Capability

3. Energised Individuals

Each component is valuable independently. Collectively they create a network that allows Teamership to thrive. Let's look at each of these in more detail, where you will see how anchors highlight the value of accelerators:

NETWORK ANCHORS	NETWORK ACCELERATORS
Lack of horizontal collaboration	Connected Leadership Teams
Rigid policies and procedures	Dynamic Leadership Capability
Burnout or "quiet quitting"	Energised individuals

CONNECTED LEADERSHIP
TEAMS

Connected Leadership Teams play an important role in supporting Teamership – highly visible leadership teams that are connected to the organisation's vision, to each other and throughout the organisation act as a key promoter of Teamership behaviours. They model behaviour and create an environment that allows members to be a part of a committed team. At the same time, they are experiencing and learning about how to be a part of a high performance team. Members of Connected Leadership Teams can share these lessons and experiences across the multiple teams they belong to.

Too often, leadership teams are viewed as administrative functions that exist only on the organisational chart. Members of leadership teams view their *real role* as leading the team or function that they are the appointed to head. They don't see that working together is a valuable use of their energy, attention, and time.

This is a huge risk. In fact, Geoff Martin, Professor of Strategy at Melbourne Business School, recently told me that there is consistent evidence that suggests that:

" *The #1 reason that strategy fails is a lack of horizontal collaboration.* "

Geoff Martin
Professor of Strategy at Melbourne Business School

That stopped me in my tracks. Leadership teams need to be better connected to deliver on their strategic objectives, to foster a culture aligned with their values and to support Teamership.

In the context of Teamership, organisations benefit from leadership teams that are connected in three distinct and complementary ways:

- Connected to the organisation purpose, strategy and vision
- Connected to each other as humans, not resources
- Connected throughout and beyond the organisation.

SENIOR LEADERSHIP NEEDS TO TEAM UP

When leaders are a part of Connected Leadership Teams, they are able to add value in all of the teams that they are a part of. There are benefits for everyone:

- The work becomes more rewarding for the individual leaders.
- The teams that they contribute to lift their performance.
- Organisations collaborate better cross-functionally.

Simply bringing together a group of talented, hard working and dedicated leaders is not enough. What is required involves acknowledging that teams are more than a group of skilled people thrown together. Teams require a way of working that allows them to produce something better together than they could create independently.

Investing in high performing leadership teams is a point of leverage worthy of consideration for organisations. It develops leaders who are better able to operate in complexity, teams that are better able to collaborate and ultimately provide organisations with a sustainable competitive advantage.

The Team Performance System is a deliberate approach that takes leadership development and performance development from an event into a way of working. My first book, *Team Up*, explores how to take a deliberate approach to team performance in more detail through the lens of the Team Performance System. This system shows that a team's performance is the product of its capability, cohesion and context:

TEAM PERFORMANCE SYSTEM

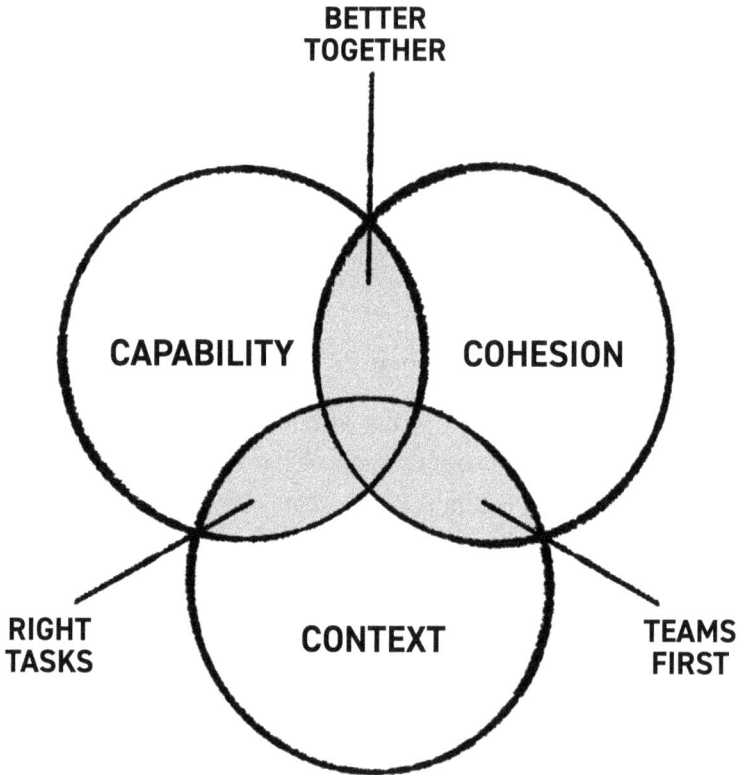

- Capability: The ability of team members to perform tasks.

- Cohesion: How well team members can work together to perform tasks.

- Context: The circumstances and setting for the team.

When teams are able to operate with high levels of capability, cohesion and context, team members can take actions that are the right tasks, performed better together and prioritise the needs of the team over individual needs.

DYNAMIC LEADERSHIP
CAPABILITY ∞

Dynamic leadership capability extends the capacity and likelihood of high levels of Teamership. By dynamic, I don't mean charismatic. There is danger in relying too heavily on the personality of leaders to charm others. By dynamic, I mean the ability of leaders to operate in a range of ways in response to the context of their teams and the broader organisation. It centres upon leadership with behavioural flexibility.

Dynamic leadership has the behavioural flexibility to adapt and respond to the needs of the team and the team's context, and not an individual's leadership preferences. Behavioural flexibility being demonstrated by leaders, models and mirrors the value of team members who are able to respond appropriately in different situations. The actions of leaders are far more significant than their words, so a congruence between what leaders expect of themselves and others is a powerful signal. In the same way, incongruent actions undermine a message's effectiveness.

Leading in a multiple team network also requires a constant awareness of a team's context, that is, the team's members, purpose, and the circumstances within which it operates. None of these elements is stable or fixed. They are all dynamic in the sense that they are *continuously changing or developing*.

Dynamic leadership creates the space for leadership to emerge and develop from all team members and is strengthened – not threatened – by team members taking leadership responsibilities. Teamership is accelerated by leadership that is dynamic and responsive, able to share information rapidly, experiment, learn and empower others.

DYNAMIC LEADERS NEED TO SEE AND BE SEEN

Leaders who have all the answers fast run out of value. In situations where there are clear answers, there is limited value in leadership. Those situations can be resolved through management and implementation of a technical solution. Leadership is of most value in ambiguity – and that's where we need our leaders to show up.

More often than not, effective leadership is the cumulative product of small, human interactions that build real connections. Connections that go beyond transactions. High quality connections are the only way that a network can be greater than the sum of its parts. Dynamic leaders show up in the places that matter in a way that makes a difference to build, maintain and strengthen connections. That allows them to access the collective intelligence of those that they work with to better understand and operate in ambiguity.

At its core, dynamic leadership requires two things of leaders:

1. TO SEE ...

When leaders see the environment, the people, and the circumstances in which they are operating, they can add value. This assumes leaders are not hiding behind emails, policies, jargon, and boss-pleasers who tell them what they want to hear. It also needs leaders who are present, engaged, and prefer truth to convenience.

2. TO BE SEEN ...

A leader seeing and engaging with reality is helpful. This is amplified by leaders who allow themselves to be seen. Leaders who share their strengths, weaknesses, challenges, concerns, and failures are not only reducing the mental load of leadership, they also make it easier for others to do the same and be seen themselves.

We don't need heroes as leaders. We need humans who are able to see and be seen. Teamership needs leaders that Show Up.

ENERGISED INDIVIDUALS

Energised individuals are both a cause and a symptom of an environment that drives Teamership. High levels of Teamership go hand-in-hand with individual members being energised and energising. This allows individuals to bring their best.

Being around individuals who participate with optimism, motivation, and vigour encourages others to do the same. This supports bringing out the best in others.

For Teamership, 'energy' applies a specific definition from Rob Cross and others at Ross Business School in Michigan. It refers to how employees are "mentally engaged, enthused and willing to commit efforts to possibilities" while engaging in their work. Through this lens, the difference between individuals being energised, or not, is difficult to overstate.

An Oxford Review research briefing on relational energy cited research findings that positive energy significantly increases an individual's:

- Resources

- Resilience

- Resourcefulness

- Creativity

- Flexibility

- Productivity

- Learning capacity.

In addition to individual productivity, there are other gains that benefit teams and organisations. Positive energy reduces the impacts of stress, increases employee engagement and job satisfaction.

It's difficult to overstate the impact that energised individuals have. All of these findings make it more likely that an individual will be able to *bring their best work*. A key implication is also that energy is transmitted between individuals. This means that positive relational energy is an important way to help *bring out the best in others*.

THE MINDSETS OF ENERGISED INDIVIDUALS

We have discussed how Teamership is an adaptive challenge – one that requires a shift in both mindsets and skillsets.

Mindset has become a bit of a buzzword in academia and popular business conversation since the great work of Professor

Carol Dweck gained notoriety. Her book, *Mindset*, focused on the benefit of a growth mindset, particularly for learning and improving performance. Ironically, however, the focus on the value of growth mindsets may have underplayed the impact of mindsets more broadly. In the context of our discussion, I am applying a broader lens to mindset.

Cambridge Dictionary defines mindset as:

"a person's way of thinking and their opinions"

For Energised Individuals, it is evident that a person's *way of thinking and their opinions* will affect the extent to which they are *mentally engaged, enthused and willing to commit efforts to possibilities*, which is how relational energy has been defined.

Four specific mindsets enable Teamership at an individual level:

- Awareness
- Adaptability
- Ambition
- Agency.

Applying these mindsets and their associated skillsets – which we will explore shortly – allows individuals to be both energised and energising in their roles on multiple teams.

When applying these skillsets and mindsets, there are a few important points to keep in mind. First, the skillsets I am referring to are a cluster of capabilities. For example, self-awareness incorporates mindfulness, reflective practices, seeking feedback, listening and questioning. Secondly, there are more ways to positively contribute to collective performance than there are people on the planet. Thirdly, these skillsets and mindsets are in the context of relational energy, which is independent of an individual's technical capability.

There are infinite ways to be an energised and energising team member. I would not want to discourage or limit the ways that individuals can contribute to collective performance. Sometimes when making choices about where to start, the possibilities can be overwhelming, like choosing what to watch on Netflix. The intent of the selected mindsets and skillsets is to provide a framework for individuals, leaders, teams and organisations to explore and develop Teamership.

ENERGISED INDIVIDUALS NEED AWARENESS

Great team members have great awareness. That involves staying present to the context in which they are operating. The skillsets – clusters of capabilities – that are most directly connected to the mindset of awareness in the context of Teamership are:

- Self-awareness
- Team awareness
- System awareness

ENERGISED INDIVIDUALS NEED ADAPTABILITY

Awareness of a situation is helpful. It is amplified when it is combined with the ability to adjust behaviour according to changing demands. The capacity for behavioural flexibility is useful in most team settings and particularly valuable in multiple team environments.

The skillsets that are connected with a mindset of Adaptability are the ability to:

- Play On
- Engage in Dialogue
- Create better connections

ENERGISED INDIVIDUALS NEED AMBITION

A common misconception of being a great team member is that it's fluffy. That it is somehow soft and occurs at the expense of high performance. That is not the case and is exemplified by the third mindset of Teamership – Ambition. Teamership promotes many of the behaviours that are the antidote of mediocrity such as boldness, without compromising wellbeing, growth, and relationships.

The skillsets connected with Ambition are:

- Fostering motivation
- Innovation
- Level up

ENERGISED INDIVIDUALS NEED AGENCY

Albert Bandura was a widely respected researcher in psychology. He wrote extensively on a range of issues, including agency. Applying concepts from a 2006 paper by Bandura, people who adopt a mindset of Agency "are not simply onlookers of their behaviour. They are contributors to their life circumstances, not just products of them".

For the purposes of Teamership, it is valuable to consider agency through the skillsets of:

- Accountability
- Generosity
- Proactivity

To explore these skillsets and mindsets in more detail, visit teamership.com.au/resources or use the QR code.

ENERGISED INDIVIDUALS BRING THEIR BEST AND BRING OUT THE BEST IN OTHERS.

REFLECTIVE QUESTIONS

To help you bring your best

These questions are designed to help you to consider how you can better bring your best to the teams that you are part of, particularly considering ways to design Teamership as a part of your ways of working. Considering these will help you to be more energised and energising.

1. What are you like at your best?

2. When do you bring your best to your teams?

3. What do you do to bring out the best in others?

4. How do others bring out the best in you?

5. Have you noticed anything that makes it hard for you to bring your best?

6. Do you ever inadvertently hide your best work?

7. What are some things that energise you?

8. How do you positively impact the energy of others?

9. Are there things that drain your energy?

10. Do you ever negatively impact the energy of others?

DISCUSSION GUIDE

To help bring out the best in others

For Leadership Teams

1. Is a lack of horizontal collaboration limiting our strategic effectiveness?

2. How well are members of our team connected to each other?

3. How well is our team connected to our mission, purpose and values?

4. How well is our team connected throughout and beyond the organisation?

5. Are we supporting the 75% of teams that are not on our org chart?

6. Do we role model the behaviours that support a more collaborative, resilient and performance focused organisation?

For established and emerging leaders

7. How well do we operate dynamically in response to changing needs?

8. Where are the important places for us to show up as leaders?

9. How do we want to show up as leaders in the places that make a difference?

10. What helps us to better see the environment, the people and the circumstances with which we are operating?

11. What makes it hard for us to see the environment, the people and the circumstances with which we are operating?

12. Is there a way we can better support each other?

SECTION V

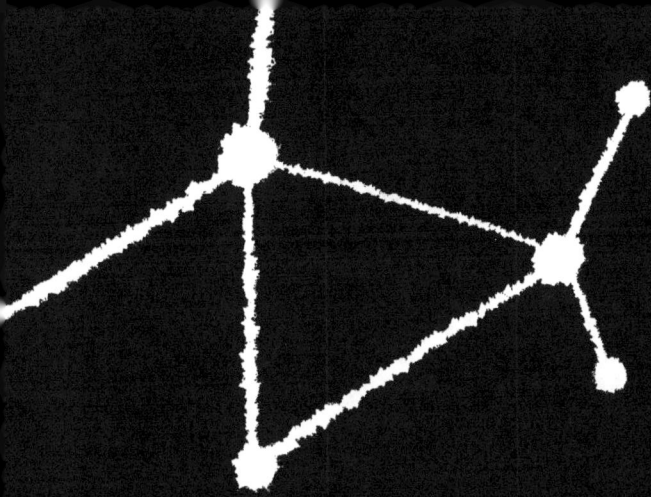

INTEGRATING
TEAMERSHIP

Establish Escape Velocity.

Start where you are.
Do what you can.

Start a food diary.

Apply the Serengeti Rules.

Identify the keystone people.

Promote and support
keystone behaviours.

Reflection and Inflection.

ONE WAY to think about behaviour change is that it exists in a cycle from inertia through to integration. The midway stages are inspiration and implementation. Inspiration is the desire to change. Implementation is putting those changes into practice. Integration is making those practices a seamless part of functioning.

Each stage, from inspiration to implementation and integration, is important and builds on the preceding stages. There is also increased longevity with each stage. Inspiration is great but won't last long if it doesn't lead to implementation. Implementation is necessary but will require too much effort to maintain unless we find a way to achieve integration. Integration is what is required to make any behaviour change a long-term shift.

Integrating Teamership at any level – individual, team or organisation – involves committing to Teamership, designing Teamership and ultimately embedding Teamership practices and principles into ways of working. The reason this is so important can be summarised by Holzwarth's first law of human behaviour published via behavioraleconomics.com, which states that:

Behaviour tends to follow the status quo unless it is acted upon by a decrease in friction or increase in fuel.

This is, in essence, about behavioural inertia – we will continue to do what we have done until something makes another behaviour more likely. That can happen because we are more motivated or the behaviour has become easier.

This is an example of the status quo bias and is directly applicable in our Teamership.

The status quo is based on the assumption that organisations are static hierarchies of resources that can be managed mechanically. The status quo may not be what we need or even want, but the first law reminds us that the status quo has power – it is familiar, comfortable, safe, and it got us to where we are even when innovation is necessary in the long run. What could possibly be bad about the status quo?

The problem is that organisations need to be dynamic networks of humans that think systemically and in the long run, innovation is essential. A bias for the status quo will not let you achieve what is required now or into the future.

For those of us who see the value in Teamership and are seeking to help ourselves and others bring their best, we need to find ways to make Teamership a part of who we are and how we operate.

This section examines:

- The energy required to shift the status quo.

- Ways to identify the people and behaviours that will drive integration.

- Tips on maintaining practices and principles of Teamership in your ways of working.

ESTABLISH ESCAPE VELOCITY

NASA talks about escape velocity as *the speed at which an object must travel to escape a planet or moon's gravitational pull.*

Apparently, achieving escape velocity is one of the biggest challenges facing space travel. Sending rockets to space is physics. In the context of Teamership, escape velocity is a useful metaphor.

Overcoming the gravitational pull of the status quo is just as challenging as exiting a planet's gravitational pull. The forces that keep us working in certain ways are powerful. They have been implemented and reinforced for centuries and are designed into the assumptions that organisations have been built on.

For both rockets and progressive organisations, escape velocity is crucial to success and initially energy intensive. To escape gravitational pull, an object needs to be travelling fast enough for long enough to no longer be drawn towards the planet or moon. The payoff is significant. Once it has achieved escape velocity, the object has much more freedom. Without the pull of gravitational forces, it could, but does not need to, return to the planet.

Perhaps it will even be able to move beyond orbit, free to explore more directions or decide to voyage into the gravitational field of another planet or body.

The most important thing to recognise when we are looking to shift how we work as organisations is that making such changes takes effort and attention at the right pace over a sustained period. Many leaders, teams and organisations have a genuine intent to change how they work, but unless they generate enough momentum to overcome the gravitational forces from both inside and outside the organisation that led them to their current ways of working, they will return to the status quo sooner or later.

START WHERE YOU ARE.
DO WHAT YOU CAN.

It is valuable to make a distinction between simple and easy.
The objective of a marathon is simple – run 42.2km.
But clearly, achieving that objective is anything but easy.

Like running a marathon, the objective of Teamership is
straightforward. The objective boils down to two simple
questions, the answers to which are complex:

Am I bringing my best?
Am I bringing out the best in others?

What does it take for any of us to know ourselves well enough
to understand what our best could be? It is possible that we
will never fully know the answer to that. If we can't answer that
question of ourselves, how can we answer it for another person,
let alone in the context of multiple teams?

If that wasn't hard enough, how can we expect to help others to
answer these questions while we are wrestling so hard with them
ourselves?

My recommendation is simple, though not easy to achieve. It is to acknowledge the complexity of the challenge by applying adaptive solutions. Teamership is not something that will be quickly solved or a box that will be ticked through a technical solution. Supporting Teamership is a decision, an ongoing commitment in service of yourself, those you work with, and those who rely on the work that your organisation does.

To do this you need to *start where you are and do what you can.*

Without trying to be too zen about it, this is all we are ever able to do. You can't start from anywhere other than where you are, and you can't do more than you can! The trick is to acknowledge both of those things.

Where are you, your leaders, your teams and your organisation? Start there.

What can you do to help, support, promote and invest in Teamership? Do that.

START A FOOD DIARY

Part of the effectiveness of food diaries in changing behaviour is that they change what we pay attention to. When a dietitian asks their client to keep a food diary, the client makes better food choices. The diary helps to shift inspiration to implementation.

I have experienced a version of this myself. My cousin Robynne is a dietitian and I have engaged her support a few times. The fact that I have to report back to her on what I eat makes it far less likely that I will have a slice of banana bread and more likely that I will choose to eat a banana. This is reinforced any time that my wife Rebecca tells me that banana bread is far more like *banana cake* than either banana or bread.

You can apply these principles to your benefit when it comes to Teamership. Find a way to pay more attention to your behaviours and those of others. Identify the things that are making a positive contribution to collective performance. It makes it even better if you do this with others, for two reasons:

1. The fact that you have committed to sharing your reflections with others will make you more likely to complete the task.

2. You are making it more likely that others will also pay increased attention to Teamership in their roles.

This is a way of starting where you are and doing what you can. You are doing the former by identifying current levels of performance and simultaneously doing the latter without the need for a significant investment of time, energy or resources. Having an increased focus on Teamership will help to improve performance behaviours in the same way that food diaries improve eating by committing attention to the desired behaviours.

APPLY THE _____ SERENGETI RULES

For a recent family movie night, I bucked the trend of watching comedies, animated films, or family friendly dramas to watch ... a documentary.

The film was called *The Serengeti Rules* and is based on the book by Sean B. Carroll of the same title. Apologies for the minor spoilers here – I still enjoyed a second watching, so I don't think I'm taking away from your experience too much if you decide to watch it.

The Serengeti Rules tells the story of a group of researchers who independently explored a range of ecosystems, ranging from tidal pools to kelp forests, rainforests and, of course, the Serengeti. What ties the researchers together are the same connecting principles that allow each of those systems to thrive or diminish. They referred to a thriving ecosystem as one that is upgrading, and a diminishing ecosystem as one that is downgrading.

Initially, the lead researcher believed that the key to ecosystems that can reverse the process of downgrading and lead to upgrading was dependent upon predators.

He believed the predators helped to keep other populations in balance. This view became more nuanced and led to a view about trophic cascades which, according to the film's website, is:

> *"a phenomenon where species impact other species even if there are no direct interactions among them."*

In an organisational setting, we are all continually setting off trophic cascades. The way that we work with our team affects the way in which members participate on other projects, which impacts how our clients experience our organisation, which influences our Chief Financial Officer's job in forecasting cashflow, which affects how many people the company can hire ... and so on. This is how complex adaptive systems work. Every action is connected either directly, loosely or indirectly with other parts of the system and contributes to the system's functioning.

The Serengeti Rules researchers' breakthrough was taking the logic of trophic cascades one step further. It was identifying the species that had the most significant impact through trophic cascades. The term that they used was keystone species, which is one that has an "outsized influence on an ecosystem and if it were removed the ecosystem would change drastically."

The researchers in the film found that these keystone species varied from setting to setting. For example, sea otters, starfish, and wildebeest were each keystones in their environments. Subsequent research has identified that they can be spiders or even plants, as long as that species has a disproportionate impact on the systems in which it operates. In the context of Teamership, rather than being species, the keystones are people and behaviours.

IDENTIFY THE _____ KEYSTONE PEOPLE

A quote often attributed to anthropologist Margaret Mead encourages readers to 'never doubt that a small group of thoughtful, committed citizens can change the world; indeed, it's the only thing that ever has'.

Regardless of the origin of the quote – there is some conjecture about whether Mead said or wrote it – the message is relevant: behavioural change, particularly involving large groups of people, is not a linear process, or a binary on/off switch. It is a gradual process that happens over time, that starts small and grows from there.

Looking at different behavioural or organisational change models, a few common themes appear:

- There are stages to the process
- Not everyone will be on board at first
- Things often go backwards before they go forwards
- Change efforts take effort!

As much as we know that not everyone will be on board as soon as we think it's a good idea, it is easy to fall into one (or both) of the following traps:

1. We want everyone to share our enthusiasm or perspective on the change.

2. We target specific people to be advocates and drive change.

So how do you identify the thoughtful, committed keystone citizens who will support you to integrate Teamership into your workplace? I suggest two steps, which can be used independently or together:

1. FIND THE BELIEVERS

Seth Godin is an author and marketing expert. He has an incredible record of engaging and enrolling others to support ideas that he believes in. His advice is to "Shun the non-believers. Ignore the well-meaning but unmoved. Instead, we have the chance to find and connect and celebrate the people who care enough to make a difference."

Rather than shunning the non-believers, I prefer to think of it as finding the believers. The good news is that you might need fewer believers than you think. Godin suggests that "if 2% of a population takes coordinated action, it makes a difference. If 5% do, it can change everything."

2. LISTEN TO THE KEYSTONES

It may be that there are specific people in your organisation that you want to engage. For example, in an established hierarchy or matrix organisation, senior leadership has a disproportionate influence on the organisation or perhaps there are other influential people within the organisation that you would like to enrol in your efforts.

As tempting as it may be to tell them about your ideas, I'd recommend listening to their desires, hopes, concerns and aspirations. If Teamership aligns to their perspectives, you have an opportunity to share Teamership through the lens of what they value. That is more likely to lead to their support with inspiration, implementation and ultimately, integration.

PROMOTE AND SUPPORT KEYSTONE BEHAVIOURS

As you are paying more attention to Teamership, you will be able to identify behaviours that can have a disproportionate influence on team and organisational performance. Those behaviours may change from setting to setting and identifying patterns will allow you to share what you are learning with others, as well as promote and support those behaviours. A few simple ways to do that are by:

1. PROVIDING FEEDBACK TO PEOPLE WHEN YOU NOTICE IT. FOR EXAMPLE ...

"Hey Jane, I just noticed that you asked a few really useful questions in that meeting. I think that allowed the team to consider a few options they hadn't previously looked at and allowed Jo to share their experience. Thanks!"

2. ROLE MODELING THE BEHAVIOURS THAT YOU HAVE NOTICED

In this example, after noticing that Jane asked good questions, you could make a deliberate effort to increase and improve the questions that you ask in your meetings. This will demonstrate the behavioural patterns that you have observed being helpful.

3. RUN EXPERIMENTS AND SHOW YOUR WORK IN PROGRESS

A hugely undervalued approach for engaging and empowering others is to share your thinking. It is just like in high school maths, where you get partial marks for showing your working even if the answer is wrong. You can encourage behaviours simply by disclosing your thinking. For example ...

"I've noticed Jane asking some great questions recently that have helped us get to better outcomes, so you might notice me trying to incorporate questions more often."

REFLECTION AND INFLECTION

Towards the end of a session or program with leaders or a team, I often facilitate a discussion designed to provide a lasting benefit for all those in the room.

The format changes from session to session but the intent remains the same, which is for participants to consider what meaning they can take away from the session based on their work context. Once they have done that, they can decide on what actions they would like to take as a result of the program. The phrase that I have landed on is Reflection and Inflection. So now we have reached the end of the book, I would like you to find the lasting benefit that you will take away from your reading.

REFLECTION

The first step is to look back on what you've read and consider the following questions:

1. What comes up for you as you reflect on the themes of the book?

2. What can you remember?

3. What has resonated with you?

4. What meaning did you make of what you read?

5. What are you curious to know more about?

INFLECTION

The second step is to look forward. My great wish is that this book provides you with both a call to action and a path to action for you to bring your best and bring out the best in others. Identify what you need – whether it is inspiration, evidence, a framework, or a point of reference – by considering the following questions:

1. What would you like to do differently?

2. What would you like to do more?

3. What would you like to do less?

4. How will you implement practices of Teamership?

5. What will help you to move beyond implementation to integration?

And finally, I hope this leaves you with the tools to answer the main question ...

How will you use this book to bring your best and bring out the best in others?

GRATITUDE

Finally, let me say a direct and sincere thanks to you.

I wanted this book to be as succinct as possible because I know that many other things compete for your energy, attention, and time. I am deeply grateful that you have chosen to give your attention to this book – and have made it to the end.

I also wanted to keep the messages clear.

I believe deeply that being a great team member is who we are at our best – individually and collectively.

I believe that being a great team member is as important as it is challenging.

I believe that supporting each other to be great team members is its own reward.

I believe that this work matters.

If that is true for you, then I hope that this book has provided you with both a call to action and a path to action.

I hope that you will start where you are and do what you can.

I hope that you will share what you learn – including the things that don't work.

I hope that you will bring your best.

I hope that you will bring out the best in others.

REFERENCES

ARTICLES

Almaatouq, A., Alsobay, M., Yin, M. and Watts, D.J., 2021. 'Task complexity moderates group synergy.' Proceedings of the National Academy of Sciences, 118(36), p.e2101062118.

Bandura, A., 2006. 'Toward a psychology of human agency.' Perspectives on psychological science, 1(2), pp.164-180.

Buckingham, M. and Goodall, A., 2019. 'The power of hidden teams.' Harvard Business Review, 20(2), pp.1-18.

Cross, R., Baker, W. and Parker, A., 2003. 'What creates energy in organizations?' MIT Sloan Management Review, 44(4), p.51.

D'Innocenzo, L., Mathieu, J.E. and Kukenberger, M.R., 2016. 'A meta-analysis of different forms of shared leadership–team performance relations.' Journal of Management, 42(7), pp.1964-1991.

Heifetz, R.A. and Linsky, M., 2002. 'A survival guide for leaders.' Harvard business review, 80(6), pp.65-74.

Lewin, K., 1943. 'Defining the 'field at a given time'.' Psychological Review, 50(3), p.292.

Margolis, J., 2020. 'Multiple team membership: An integrative review.' Small Group Research, 51(1), pp.48-86.

Martin, A. and Bal, V., 2015. The state of teams [White paper].

Mathieu, J.E., Gallagher, P.T., Domingo, M.A. and Klock, E.A.,

2019. Embracing complexity: Reviewing the past decade of team effectiveness research. Annual Review of Organizational Psychology and Organizational Behavior, 6, pp.17-46.

Mortensen, M. and Gardner, H.K., 2017. 'The overcommitted organization.' Harvard Business Review, 95(5), pp.58-65.

O'leary, M.B., Mortensen, M. and Woolley, A.W., 2011. 'Multiple team membership: A theoretical model of its effects on productivity and learning for individuals and teams.' Academy of Management Review, 36(3), pp.461-478.

O'Neill, T.A. and Salas, E., 2018. 'Creating high performance teamwork in organizations.' Human resource management review, 28(4), pp.325-331.

Peterson, R.S. and Behfar, K., 2022. 'When to cooperate with colleagues and when to compete.' Harvard Business Review.

Shuffler, M.L., Jiménez-Rodríguez, M. and Kramer, W.S., 2015. 'The science of multiteam systems: A review and future research agenda.' Small Group Research, 46(6), pp.659-699.

Taylor, B., 2010. 'Brand is culture, culture is brand.' Harvard Business Review, 27.

Volini, E., Schwartz, J., Roy, I., Hauptmann, M., Van Durme, Y., Denny, B. and Bersin, J., 2019. 'Leading the social enterprise: Reinvent with a human focus.' Deloitte Global Human Capital Trends.

Westrum, R., 2004. 'A typology of organisational cultures.' BMJ Quality & Safety, 13(suppl 2), pp.ii22-ii27.

'Relational Energy: what it is and why it matters to organisations.', In The Oxford Review Encyclopaedia of Terms. Research Briefing. The Oxford Review. www.oxford-review. com [Accessed 12 October 2022]

BOOKS

Grant, A., 2014. Give and take: Why helping others drives our success. Penguin.

Hayes, M., Chumney, F., Wright, C. and Buckingham, M., 2019. Global study of engagement. ADP Research.

Kellerman, B., 2008. How followers are creating change and changing leaders. Boston, MA: Harvard Business School.

Mankins, M.C. and Garton, E., 2017. Time, Talent, Energy: Overcome Organizational Drag and Unleash Your Team s Productive Power. Harvard Business Review Press.

Thaler, R.H. and Sunstein, C.R., 2009. Nudge: Improving decisions about health, wealth, and happiness. Penguin.

Van Nieuwerburgh, C., 2016. Interculturally-sensitive coaching. The Sage handbook of coaching, pp.439-452.

Wageman, R., Nunes, D.A., Burruss, J.A. and Hackman, J.R., 2008. Senior leadership teams: What it takes to make them great. Harvard Business Review Press.

Yukl, G.A., 2013. Leadership in organizations (Global ed.). Essex: Pearson.

WEBSITES

https://barbarakellerman.com/the-normalization-of-followership/ [Accessed 12 October 2022]

https://cambridge-leadership.com/principles/ [Accessed 12 October 2022]

www.mckinsey.com. (n.d.). To weather a crisis, build a network of teams. https://www.mckinsey.com/capabilities/people-and-organizational-performance/our-insights/to-weather-a-crisis-build-a-network-of-teams [Accessed 12 October 2022].

https://www.macquarie.com.au/perspective/case-studies/the-impossible-institute-behaviour-by-design.html [Accessed 12 October 2022]

https://pressbooks.lib.vt.edu/strategicmanagement/chapter/4-3-resource-based-view/ [Accessed 12 October 2022]

https://www.behavioraleconomics.com/the-three-laws-of-human-behavior/ [Accessed 12 October 2022]

https://seths.blog/2022/05/the-ones-who-didnt-help/ [Accessed 12 October 2022]

https://www.inc.com/marcel-schwantes/bill-gates-explains-what-separates-successful-leaders-from-everyone-else-in-2-words.html [Accessed 12 October 2022]

https://www.theserengetirules.com/science [Accessed 12 October 2022]

https://www.nasa.gov/audience/foreducators/k-4/features/F_Escape_Velocity.html [Accessed 12 October 2022]

CONTINUE THE CONVERSATION

As Morpheus told us in *The Matrix*, there is a difference between knowing the path and walking the path. I work with leaders, teams and organisations to help them walk the path and apply the principles of *Teamership*. If you would like to explore how my speaking, coaching, facilitation, or training offerings, get in touch and let's chat!

www.keeganluiters.com

keegan@keeganluiters.com

LinkedIn: Keegan Luiters

I look forward to continuing the conversation,

Keegan

TEAMERSHIP MANIFESTO

Teamership is not followership.

Teamership is a form of leadership.

Teamership is a competitive advantage.

Teamership is the product of two questions.

Teamership is a commitment to making together better.

Teamership is a choice.

Your org chart is lying to you.

Shifting to a team-based network model
improves performance.

93% of organisations aren't ready
to operate as networks.

The rise of multiple team members.

Individuals on multiple teams are overcommitted.

Teamership impacts culture and vice versa.

Teamership supports collaboration.

Teamership supports resilience.

Teamership promotes shared leadership.

Teamership prioritises learning.

Teamership is an untapped energy source.

Behaviour is a function of the person
and their environment.

Teamership is an adaptive challenge.

An organisational network needs
a Teamership network.

Teamership needs Connected Leadership Teams.

Teamership needs Dynamic Leadership Capability.

Teamership needs Energised Individuals.

Energised Individuals bring their best
and bring out the best in others.

Establish Escape Velocity.

Start where you are. Do what you can.

Apply the Serengeti Rules.

Identify the keystone people.

Promote and support keystone behaviours.

www.ingramcontent.com/pod-product-compliance
Lightning Source LLC
Chambersburg PA
CBHW071904200326
41519CB00016B/4504